The Best Of Today's

MOVIE THEMES

Project Manager: TONY ESPOSITO

Contents

Theme from "UP CLOSE & PERSONAL"

BECAUSE YOU LOVED ME

Words and Music by
DIANE WARREN
Arranged by TONY ESPOSITO

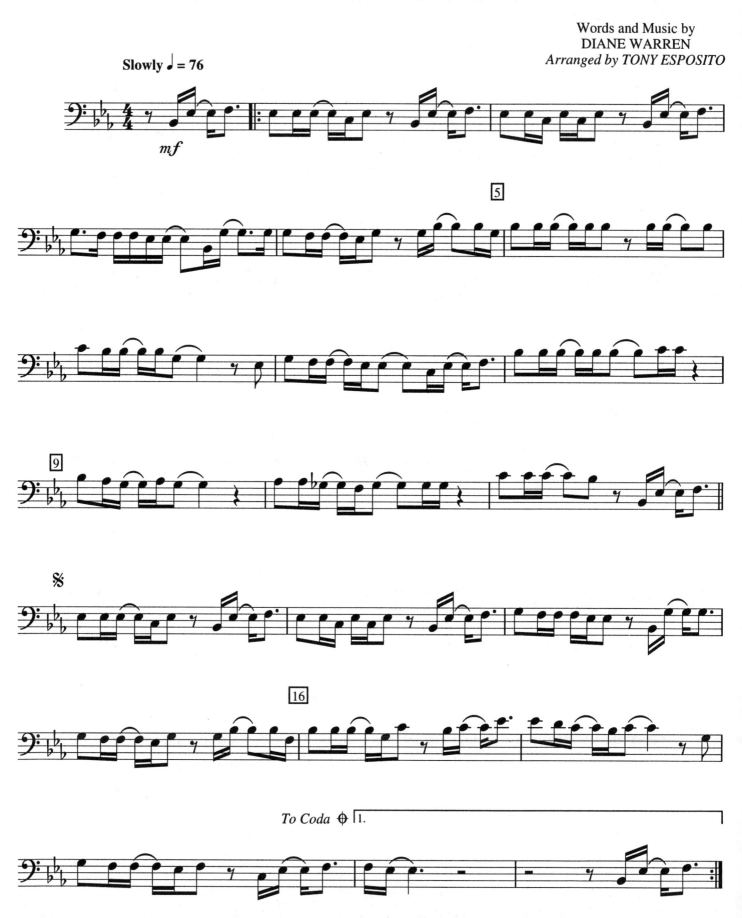

Because You Loved Me - 2 - 1
IF9819

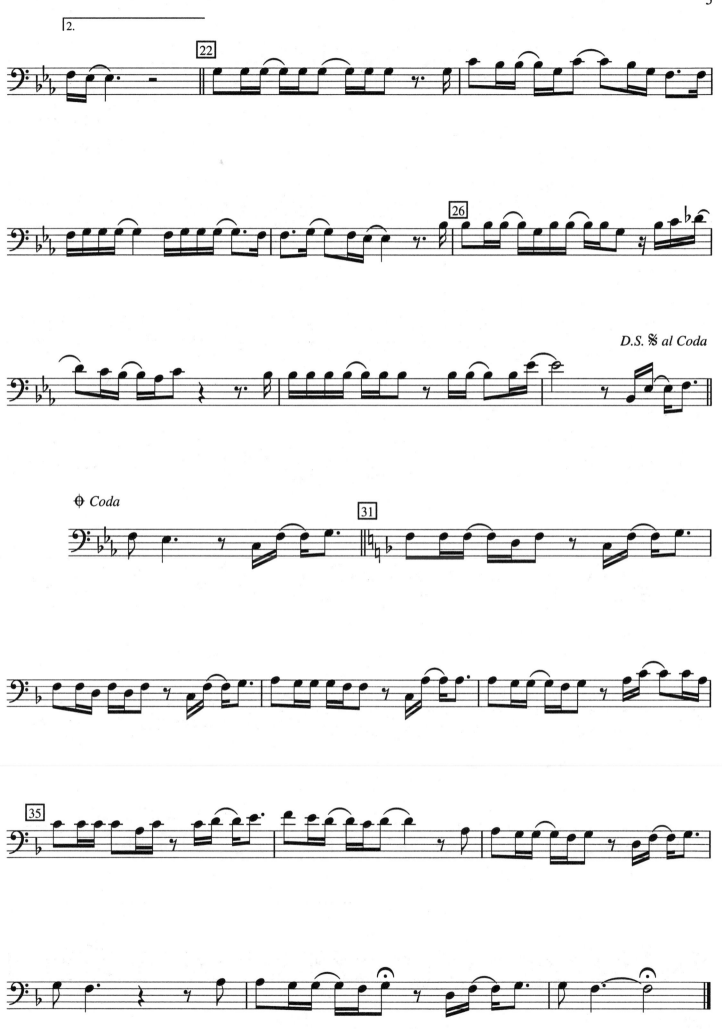

From the Lucasfilm Ltd. Production "STAR WARS" - A Twentieth Century-Fox Release.

CANTINA BAND

Music by
JOHN WILLIAMS
Arranged by TONY ESPOSITO

From the Lucasfilm Ltd. Productions "STAR WARS", "THE EMPIRE STRIKES BACK"
and "RETURN OF THE JEDI" - Twentieth Century-Fox Releases.

STAR WARS
(Main Theme)

Music by
JOHN WILLIAMS
Arranged by TONY ESPOSITO

FOOLISH GAMES

By JEWEL KILCHER
Arranged by TONY ESPOSITO

IF9819

From Warner Bros. "QUEST FOR CAMELOT"

THE PRAYER

Words and Music by
CAROLE BAYER SAGER and DAVID FOSTER
Arranged by TONY ESPOSITO

FOR YOU I WILL

Words and Music by
DIANE WARREN
Arranged by TONY ESPOSITO

For You I Will - 2 - 1
IF9819

GOTHAM CITY

Words and Music by
R. KELLY
Arranged by TONY ESPOSITO

Gotham City - 2 - 1
IF9819

From the Touchstone Motion Picture "CON AIR"
HOW DO I LIVE

Words and Music by
DIANE WARREN
Arranged by TONY ESPOSITO

From Warner Bros. "QUEST FOR CAMELOT"

I STAND ALONE

Words and Music by
CAROLE BAYER SAGER,
DAVID FOSTER and STEVE PERRY
Arranged by TONY ESPOSITO

Theme from "SPACE JAM"

I BELIEVE I CAN FLY

Words and Music by
R. KELLY
Arranged by TONY ESPOSITO

I Believe I Can Fly - 2 - 1
IF9819

From the Lucasfilm Ltd. Production "THE EMPIRE STRIKES BACK" - A Twentieth Century-Fox Release.

THE IMPERIAL MARCH
(Darth Vader's Theme)

Music by
JOHN WILLIAMS
Arranged by TONY ESPOSITO

Love Theme from "ROMEO + JULIET"
KISSING YOU

Words and Music by
DES'REE and TIM ATACK
Arranged by TONY ESPOSITO

From Warner Bros. "QUEST FOR CAMELOT"

LOOKING THROUGH YOUR EYES

Words and Music by
CAROLE BAYER SAGER
and DAVID FOSTER
Arranged by TONY ESPOSITO

Looking Through Your Eyes - 2 - 1
IF9819

From the Twentieth Century Fox Motion Picture "ANASTASIA"

AT THE BEGINNING

Lyrics by
LYNN AHRENS

Music by
STEPHEN FLAHERTY
Arranged by TONY ESPOSITO

From the Twentieth Century Fox Motion Picture "ANASTASIA"
JOURNEY TO THE PAST

Words and Music by
LYNN AHRENS and STEPHEN FLAHERTY
Arranged by TONY ESPOSITO

Journey to the Past - 2 - 1
IF9819

From "BLUES BROTHERS"
SOUL MAN

Words and Music by
ISAAC HAYES and DAVID PORTER
Arranged by TONY ESPOSITO

From "BLUES BROTHERS 2000"

RESPECT

Words and Music by
OTIS REDDING
Arranged by TONY ESPOSITO

Love Theme from "TITANIC"

MY HEART WILL GO ON

Words by
WILL JENNINGS

Music by
JAMES HORNER
Arranged by TONY ESPOSITO